RIVER ADVENTURES
GANGES RIVER

Smart Apple Media

Published by Smart Apple Media
P.O. Box 3263, Mankato, Minnesota 56002
www.smartapplemedia.com

Published by arrangement with the Watts Publishing
Group LTD, London.

Design, editing, and picture research by Paul Manning
Maps by Stefan Chabluk

Library of Congress Cataloging-in-Publication Data
Manning, Paul, 1954-
  The Ganges River / Paul Manning.
     p. cm. -- (River adventures)
  Includes index.
  Summary: "Journey down India's longest river, the
Ganges, in this thrilling, informative adventure. Travel
through the Himalayan Mountains to the Indian Ocean
as you learn about the seasons and the land, as well as
the people and culture of India"--Provided by publisher.
  ISBN 978-1-59920-915-9 (library binding)
  1. Ganges River (India and Bangladesh)--Juvenile
literature. 2. Ganges River Valley (India and
Bangladesh)--Juvenile literature. I. Title.
  DS485.G25M36 2015
  915.4'1--dc23
                                        2012035417

ISBN: 978-1-59920-915-9   (library binding)
ISBN: 978-1-62588-585-2   (eBook)

Printed in the United States by CG Book Printers
North Mankato, Minnesota

PO 1732
3-2015

54321

Note to Teachers and Parents

Every effort has been made to ensure that the websites
listed on page 32 are suitable for children, that they
are of the highest educational value, and that they
contain no inappropriate or offensive material. However,
because of the nature of the Internet, it is impossible
to guarantee that the content of these sites will not be
altered. We strongly recommend that Internet access is
supervised by a responsible adult.

Key to Images

Top cover image: The Ganges at Varanasi
Main cover image: Hindu pilgrims on the Ganges
Previous page: A Royal Bengal tiger
This page: Bathing in the Ganges at Haridwar

Picture Credits

CONTENTS

A Ganges Journey

The Ganges is the longest river in India. It stretches for 1,550 miles (2,500 km). Fed by many different streams, it flows from the Himalayas in northern India to the Indian Ocean. You will follow the river from its **source** through India and Bangladesh to the Bay of Bengal.

A Life-Giving River

For thousands of years, people living on the banks of the Ganges have relied on its waters for drinking, washing, cooking, and watering their crops. The vast Ganges plain is one of the most **fertile** farming areas in the world. Its rice and wheat feed hundreds of millions of people.

▼ The Ganges plain stretches for 746 miles (1,200 km) across northern India. When the river floods, rich **silt** is left behind to feed the soil.

A Source of Water

Use of the Ganges for growing crops goes back to ancient times. Today, canal systems help to supply water to farms across the fertile Ganges valley. Because so much water is diverted, the river is less used for transport, but in West Bengal and Bangladesh, farmers still use boats to take their goods to market.

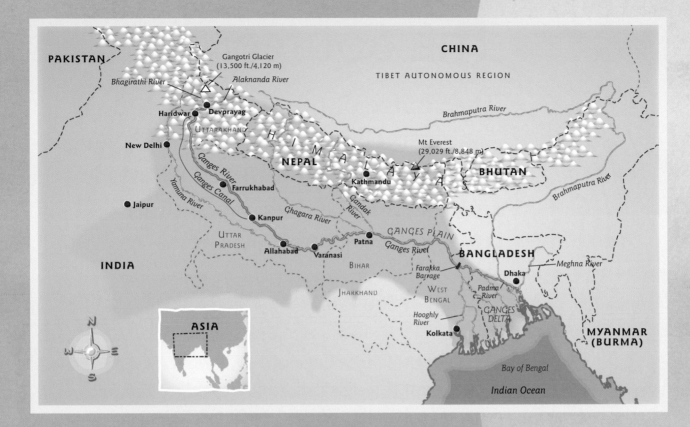

▲ Many rivers, known as **tributaries**, join the Ganges on its journey to the Indian Ocean.

A Holy River

For India's **Hindus**, the Ganges is a holy river. Its waters are believed to wash away sins. Every Hindu hopes one day to visit the holy city of Varanasi on the banks of the Ganges and bathe in the river. Each year, more than a million Hindus make this special journey, which is known as a **pilgrimage**.

▶ Washing, bathing, and praying beside the Ganges is a daily ritual for millions of Hindus.

The Source

YOU ARE HERE

The source of the Ganges is the Gangotri **Glacier** in the Himalayan Mountains. Your journey begins in this **remote** area more than 13,100 feet (4,000 m) above sea level.

▼ Snowcapped peaks tower over the Gangotri Valley in the central Himalayas.

On Top of the World

The world's highest mountain range is the Himalayas. It stretches nearly 1,865 miles (3,000 km) through Pakistan, India, Nepal, China, and Bhutan. About 100 million years ago, two gigantic plates of rock were pushed by forces below the Earth's crust. When they collided, the plates were forced upward. This massive movement created the Himalayan Mountains.

◀ The most distant tributary of the Ganges is the Bhagirathi River. It starts in this ice cave just below the Gangotri Glacier.

What Is a Glacier?

A glacier is like a frozen river. It is made from layers of snow that are packed down to form a dense mass of ice. The huge weight of the ice makes the glacier move very slowly downhill. Over thousands of years, the movement of the glacier carves out a wide U-shaped valley through the mountains.

Earthquake!

Underneath Earth's surface, the powerful forces that created the Himalayas millions of years ago are still at work today.

Sometimes, the pressure from below makes the earth tremble in a violent jolt called an earthquake. Fortunately, most earthquakes in the Himalayas occur away from towns and cities. However, in October 1991, a massive earthquake struck the town of Uttarkashi near Haridwar. It destroyed 42,000 homes and killed more than 1,000 people.

◀ This Hindu holy man has walked hundreds of miles to visit the source of the Ganges and bathe in its waters.

The High Valleys

YOU ARE HERE

Life is hard in the Himalayas. The land is covered with snow and ice for half the year. On your journey downriver, you'll meet the people who live here and farm the land.

Terraces

To create flat land for growing crops, the farmers create level areas called terraces and build stone walls to hold back the soil. The terraces collect rainwater and help to prevent soil from being washed downhill during the heavy **monsoon** rains.

▼ This Himalayan hillside has been terraced so the land can be used to grow crops.

◀ In spring and summer, meltwater and monsoon rains pour down from the mountains and swell the Ganges.

The Monsoon

Northern India lies in the path of seasonal winds called monsoons. In the monsoon season, the winds blow inland from the Indian Ocean. These winds bring tropical rainstorms that last for days and can cause heavy flooding. Nearly 80 percent of all India's rain falls during the monsoon season.

The Rainy Season

Little rain falls between November and February, and the Bhagirathi tributary flows slowly. By March, the air begins to get warm. Snow and ice start to melt in the mountains. This **meltwater** swells the river. In late June, the heavy monsoon rains arrive and the Bhagirathi becomes a raging river. Sometimes it rains so much that the river overflows its banks and floods the land.

▶ A Himalayan farmer collects feed for her cattle.

TIBET
Bhagirathi River
Devprayag
HIMALAYAS
Haridwar
New Delhi
Ganges River
INDIA
NEPAL

YOU ARE HERE

A Fragile Land

Forests on the lower slopes of the Himalayas are cleared to make way for roads, houses, mining, and farming. Trees are cut down for firewood. In places, you can see bare soil where the land has been stripped of trees.

▼ *The Bhagirathi River winds through the Himalayan* **foothills.** *Because of human activity, the forest that once covered these hills is disappearing.*

Vanishing Forest

In mountain areas, rocks and soil are constantly worn away by the weather. This is called **erosion**. Usually, erosion takes place very gradually, but when trees are cut down, the soil is suddenly left exposed.

With no tree roots to hold the soil together, it is quickly washed away by rain and ends up in the river. This raises the water level and can cause flooding.

Protecting the Forest

The villagers of the Himalayas are often blamed for cutting down trees. But fuel is scarce and other choices, such as **paraffin**, are expensive. People also need land to build houses. Farmland is too precious to use for housing, so forest is cleared instead.

Some villagers have set up tree nurseries to replant areas that have been **deforested**. Environmentalists are working with local communities to develop other sources of fuel, such as **biogas** and **solar** power, so that fewer trees need to be cut down.

▲ This hillside has been damaged by illegal dumping of mining waste.

Wildlife at Risk

When forests are cut down, many wildlife **habitats** are destroyed and animals become endangered. The forests of the Himalayas were once home to tigers, leopards, rhinoceroses, and deer. Today, these animals are found mostly in special protected areas or nature reserves.

◄ Because of habitat destruction, Himalayan species such as the snow leopard are in danger of dying out.

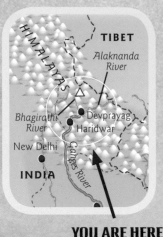

YOU ARE HERE

The Upper Ganges

Heading down from the mountains, the Bhagirathi River races over **rapids**, waterfalls, and through steep **canyons**. The roar of the water is deafening!

▼ Because of its fast-moving current, the Upper Ganges is a favorite area for whitewater rafting.

Devprayag

On its journey, the Bhagirathi is joined by other rivers. The largest tributary is the Alaknanda, which meets the river at Devprayag. This town has become a place of pilgrimage for Hindus. From here onward, the river takes the name Ganges or "Ganga."

◀ At Devprayag, the Bhagirathi River meets the Alaknanda. The name Devprayag literally means "holy meeting of the rivers."

A Haven for Wildlife

South of Devprayag, you can follow the Ganges through Rajaji National Park. This area in the Himalayan foothills was created to protect the landscape and its wildlife. The thickly wooded park is home to 50 types of mammals, including tigers, leopards, and elephants, as well as nearly 400 bird species.

In the middle of the river, four islands lie within the park boundaries. These are a rich habitat for wildlife. As you set up camp for the night, you can hear hornbills calling to each other in the trees above.

Where Rivers Meet

The place where two rivers meet is called a confluence. For Hindus, any confluence is **sacred**. The meeting of the Alaknanda and Bhagirathi at Devprayag is a holy place. The river banks are lined with stepped platforms called **ghats**. Pilgrims use the ghats to bathe in the waters of the Ganges.

▶ At Rajaji National Park, elephants come to the river to drink and bathe.

The Ganges Plain

YOU ARE HERE

At Haridwar, the Ganges River leaves the Himalayan foothills and flows across the Ganges plain. This area is almost flat, so the river moves more slowly here, except in the rainy season when the land is flooded.

▼ With its rich soils, the Ganges plain is one of the most fertile and densely populated farming areas in the world.

Farming the Floodplain

Throughout the Ganges **floodplain**, people live in small villages surrounded by fields of rice or wheat. Compared to Europe or America, the farms are tiny —about the size of two soccer fields. Many farmers grow just enough food to feed their families. Others grow crops to sell in local markets. All these people depend on the Ganges River and Ganges Canal (*see opposite*) to water their crops.

◄ A farmer and his son plow their fields with the help of a team of oxen.

As India's economy grows, young people are leaving country areas to find better-paid work in the cities. Farming methods are changing too as farmers use chemicals to help grow more crops.

A Pollution Blackspot

You reach the industrial city of Kanpur, which is 86 miles (138 km) from Farrukhabad. Along the riverbanks, factories called tanneries pour harmful chemicals into the river. This **pollution** is a real danger to people farther downstream. The Ganges also contains high levels of untreated **sewage**, so you must be sure to boil and filter any water from the river before you drink it.

▶ The Ganges Canal was built in the 1850s. Today, it supplies water to nearly 3,475 square miles (9,000 sq km) of farmland.

The Ganges Canal

Between the Ganges and the Yamuna Rivers, the Ganges Canal runs for 560 miles (900 km) through the state of Uttar Pradesh. The canal supplies water to the area known as the doab, or "land between the rivers." It also acts as storage for surplus water that falls during the monsoon season.

YOU ARE HERE

Allahabad

About 125 miles (200 km) from Kanpur, the Ganges and Yamuna Rivers meet at Allahabad. This ancient city was founded more than 4,000 years ago. Its original name, Prayaga, means "meeting of the rivers."

A City of Pilgrimage

Allahabad is a city of approximately 1.1 million people. Originally, it was an important **strategic** site, and anyone who ruled it also controlled the rivers. Today, many farmers gather here to sell their crops. The city's main industries are cotton manufacturing and food processing. For Hindus, however, it is above all a place of pilgrimage. Many thousands visit it every year to worship and pray beside the Ganges.

▼ This vast city of tents houses the millions of pilgrims who visit Allahabad during the Hindu festival of Kumbh Mela (see opposite).

▶ Hindu pilgrims bathe in the Ganges during the Kumbh Mela festival.

Kumbh Mela

The festival of Kumbh Mela is India's biggest Hindu gathering. In 2013, an estimated 100 million pilgrims took part, making it one of the largest gatherings of its kind in history.

At the climax of the festival, huge crowds gather to bathe in the river and chant the words, "Long live Mother Ganga." Pilgrims also pray, listen to sacred music, give gifts of money and food to the needy, and receive blessings from priests and holy men.

A Third River

At Allahabad, Hindus believe that the Ganges and Yamuna Rivers are joined by a third, underground river called the Saraswati. It is named after the Hindu goddess of knowledge. Ancient Hindu texts mention the Saraswati, but it has never been found. It may have been part of the Ghaggar, a dried-up river, which now only flows during the monsoon season.

YOU ARE HERE

Varanasi

About 78 miles (125 km) east of Allahabad, your journey brings you to Varanasi. During festival times, this holiest of all Indian cities is packed with pilgrims. The noise, color, and activity are overwhelming.

▼ Varanasi is a holy city. Hindus believe there is a special path to heaven at this part of the Ganges.

City of Light

Varanasi's location on the Ganges makes it very special for Hindus. For most of its course, the river flows southeast. But at Varanasi, it suddenly bends north. On the west banks of the river, the ghats face the rising sun. At dawn, these flights of stone steps are crowded with priests, pilgrims, and others who come to the river to pray.

A Hindu Funeral

At the Manikarnika Ghat, a group of **mourners** attend a Hindu funeral. After the body has been washed in holy water, it will be burned on a **pyre** of sweet-smelling **sandalwood**. The family will then scatter the ashes on the Ganges.

The Old City

Leaving the river, you head into the old city and wander through a maze of narrow alleys where shops sell silk souvenirs. Varanasi is a center of the silk industry and is famous for its beautifully colored fabrics. Other important industries are toy making, jewelry, and metalwork.

▶ There are about 100 ghats at Varanasi. These stepped bathing areas stretch for about 4 miles (6 km) along the river.

River Burial

Hindus believe that when a person's ashes are scattered on the Ganges, his or her soul will go straight to heaven. Because of the risk to health, the Indian government has tried to stop people from **cremating** bodies beside the river, but it is hard to make Hindus give up ancient customs. The practice still goes on.

YOU ARE HERE

Patna

About 160 miles (260 km) from Varanasi, you reach Patna—the capital of the State of Bihar. This historic city was once the capital of an empire covering nearly the whole of India.

A Historic Crossroads

Patna began as a small fortress overlooking the Ganges River. A city grew up around it that included palaces, gardens, temples, and markets as well as a university. Today, Patna sprawls for 10 miles (16 km) along the south bank of the Ganges. In addition to being a center of rice growing, Patna is a major river port and an important crossroads for people traveling to and from the north.

▼ The Mahatma Gandhi Setu is a bridge that links Patna in the south to northern Bihar. Approximately 3.4 miles (5.5 km), it is one of the longest river bridges in the world.

◀ Rice needs a lot of water to grow. These rice fields are fed all year by monsoon rains and water from the Ganges.

Patna Rice

Leaving the city, you visit some of the rice-growing areas in the surrounding countryside. Rice was first grown in India about 5,000 years ago. It is the country's most important crop. In many villages, you see people at work in flooded fields called paddies, harvesting the rice by hand.

While much of the rice is **consumed** at home, one variety, basmati rice, is an important export. Two-thirds of the basmati rice crop is exported, nearly a million tons.

A Vital Food

Because most Hindus do not eat meat, rice is a vital part of their diet. Most Indians eat rice at least once a day. About 600 different types of rice are grown. Rice is a source of food and income for as many as 50 million Indian households.

▶ This woman is planting rice seedlings grown in a nursery field.

The Farakka Barrage

INDIA
BIHAR
Ganges River
BANGLA-DESH
Farakka Barrage
Dhaka
Hooghly River
WEST BENGAL
Kolkata

YOU ARE HERE

Near the border with Bangladesh, the Farakka Barrage stretches across the river. This huge dam was built to divert water from the Ganges to allow big ships to travel up the Hooghly River to Kolkata.

▼ *The Farakka Barrage is one of the longest river dams in the world. It is also a road bridge for cars and trucks.*

A Controversial Dam

When the **barrage** was built in the 1970s, it caused great anger. Bangladesh accused India of stealing the Ganges's water. Since then, the two countries have shared control of the dam. This partnership is important to both countries. As populations increase, more and more people in India and Bangladesh rely on the river for fresh water, food, and transport.

◀ While some areas are affected by **drought**, others suffer catastrophic flooding. In Bihar, floods caused by heavy monsoon rains regularly swamp homes and farmland.

Whose Water?

Because of climate change, water shortages in India and Bangladesh are getting worse. Currently, India is planning to divert more water from the Ganges to drought-affected areas of Uttar Pradesh. If the plan goes ahead, it is certain to lead to more trouble between India and Bangladesh.

Effects of the Barrage

Since the barrage was built, silt from the river has become trapped behind it, causing the level of the riverbed to steadily rise. Because of this, some low-lying land in Bihar is now **waterlogged** all year round.

The dam has also stopped fish from reaching their **spawning grounds**. Several species that once lived in this stretch of the Ganges have disappeared. Because of this, many local fishermen have lost their jobs.

▶ Fishing is a vital industry for people living by the Ganges. Carp, catfish, mullet, freshwater eels, and prawns are caught in the river.

23

YOU ARE HERE

Kolkata

From Bangladesh, you cross back into India to explore the Hooghly River, which flows south toward Kolkata.

▼ Rickshaws carrying passengers and goods crowd the streets of Kolkata.

A River Port

With a total population of more than 4.5 million, Kolkata is one of the most densely populated cities in the world. Its streets are choked with traffic of every kind, from cars, taxis, and bicycle **rickshaws** to farmers carrying their produce to market in carts pulled by oxen.

Three hundred years ago, Kolkata was the gateway to east India. For 80 years, it was India's capital. Today, it is a fast-growing commercial, industrial, and financial center, and a major port.

◄ The Howrah Bridge connects Kolkata with its twin city Howrah on the opposite bank. More than a million pedestrians use the bridge each day.

Rich and Poor

With the arrival of new industries such as IT and electronics, wealth is returning to Kolkata, but many of its people are still desperately poor. Approximately 1.5 million Kolkatans live in overcrowded **slums** without **sanitation** or clean water. Many earn a living by searching the city's rubbish dumps for things they can mend, clean up, and sell.

▶ Bengali cooking is hot and spicy. These tasty fried snacks called pakoras are being cooked and sold at a Kolkata street food stall.

YOU ARE HERE

The Ganges Delta

In Bangladesh, the Ganges River is joined by the Brahmaputra River to form the Padma. This river is wide and slow moving as it winds its way to the sea.

▼ Small boats crowd the river at Dhaka, the capital of Bangladesh.

A Land of Silt

Over thousands of years, silt dropped by the Ganges, Brahmaputra, and Meghna Rivers has formed a vast area of marshy land called a delta. The Ganges Delta covers over 38,000 square miles (100,000 sq km), which is an area larger than Indiana. It is the largest river delta in the world.

◄ These Bangladeshi villagers live in makeshift shelters of bamboo and straw. They have no water supply except the rivers where they wash themselves and their animals.

The Sundarbans

Crisscrossed by narrow waterways, the Sundarbans are the largest mangrove swamps in the world. Many animals live here, including rare birds, spotted deer, tigers, crocodiles, and snakes. In Bengali, the name Sundarban means "beautiful forest."

Crowded Bangladesh

Bangladesh, where most of the delta is situated, is a crowded country that faces huge challenges. Most of its people live in small villages on low-lying land and are in constant danger from floods and tropical storms. The soils of the delta are good for growing rice and jute, and people live by catching fish. But there are few schools and hospitals in rural areas, and many people are very poor.

▶ The endangered Bengal tiger lives in the Sundarbans. The strip of swamp and forest stretches approximately 168 miles (270 km) across the delta.

YOU ARE HERE

Life in the Delta

As you explore the delta's maze of narrow rivers, you meet the people who farm and fish here. Many live on shifting islands barely 3 feet (1 m) above the tide. These people are at risk from floods and **cyclones** as well as from rising sea levels.

▼ Delta boatmen run a ferry service for villagers. With few roads, rivers are the main transport highways.

Fishing the Delta

With so much land taken up by sprawling cities, the rivers are a vital source of food. Most of the catch is freshwater fish, but some fishermen travel farther out to catch shrimps and other types of seafood. These are exported to Japan, Europe, and the United States.

◄ Farmers cut down jute stalks in a field. Once harvested, the tough jute threads are woven together to make sacks and rope.

Climate Change

Farmers of the delta need the annual monsoon rains to wash away salt and restore the soil. But too much rain can ruin crops and destroy **livestock** and homes.

While sea levels continue to rise as a result of **global warming**, the future of the delta and its people is uncertain. Experts say that sea levels could increase by as much as 1.6 feet (0.5 m) by 2100. If that happens, much of Bangladesh could be underwater.

▶ This concrete storm shelter is built on stilts to raise it above the floodwaters.

Surviving the Floods

In Bangladesh, villages are gradually becoming better prepared for floods and other natural disasters. Many now have specially built cyclone shelters where people and animals can be safe during storms and monsoon floods.

29

Glossary

barrage a type of dam used to control the flow of a river

biogas a type of fuel produced by rotting organic matter

canyon a deep, steep-sided valley

consume to eat or use

cremating the burning of a dead body

cyclone a type of tropical storm

deforestation cutting down trees, e.g., for timber or firewood

drought a time when water is very scarce

erosion the wearing away of soil or rock

fertile good for growing crops

floodplain the area affected by a river's floodwaters

foothill a smaller type of hill often found at the base of a mountain range

ghat a stepped platform for bathing

glacier a slow-moving mass of ice

global warming the rise in Earth's temperature caused by carbon gases in the atmosphere

habitat the natural home of a plant or animal

Hindu a follower of Hinduism, the main religion of India

livestock farm animals such as sheep or cows

meltwater the flow of water from melted snow or ice

monsoon a seasonal wind that brings rain

mourner a person who attends a funeral

paraffin a type of fuel often used for heating

pilgrimage a journey to a holy place

pollution chemical or waste products that harm the environment

pyre a pile of wood on which bodies are cremated

rapids a stretch of fast-flowing water

remote far away, difficult to reach

rickshaw a bicycle taxi

sacred holy

sandalwood a sweet-smelling wood used for cremation

sanitation toilets and running water

sewage human or animal waste

silt fine sediment carried downstream by a river

slum a run-down area where people live in very poor housing

solar from, or to do with, the sun, e.g., solar energy

source the place where a river begins

spawning ground a place where fish lay their eggs

strategic important for winning a fight or battle

tributary a river or stream that flows into another, larger one

waterlogged full of water

Ganges Quiz

Look up information in this book or online. Find the answers on page 32.

1 Match the captions to the pictures.

1

2

3

4

5

6

A A ferry boat on the Hooghly River

B A Macaque monkey

C A Hindu woman washing her hair by the Ganges

D Carved lions on the pillar of Ashoka at Sarnath

E Basmati rice

F A statue of the Hindu god Shiva on the banks of the Ganges

2 These places can all be found along the Ganges. Number them in order, starting with the ones nearest to the sea:

Varanasi
Devprayag
Farrukhabad
Patna
Kanpur
Allahabad
Haridwar

4 This animal is often found in the Himalayas. It is kept for its meat and milk and to carry and pull heavy loads. What is it?

3 True or false?

Bengal tigers are fierce when cornered, but hardly ever attack humans.

Websites and Further Reading

Websites

- *www.kids.nationalgeographic.com/kids/ places/find/india*
  Short introduction to India.

- *www.worldwildlife.org/species/ganges-river- dolphin*
  Fascinating facts about the Ganges river dolphin.

- *www.historyforkids.org/learn/india/religion/ hinduism.htm*
  Useful background material on Hinduism.

Further Reading

Aloian, Molly. *The Ganges: India's Sacred River* (Rivers around the World). Crabtree Pub. Co., 2010.

Rice, Earle. *The Ganges River* (Rivers of the World). Mitchell Lane Pub., 2012.

Spilsbury, Richard. *Living on the Ganges River* (World Cultures). Raintree, 2007.

Index

Answers to Ganges Quiz

1 1D, 2B, 3A, 4F, 5E, 6C. **2** Patna, Varanasi, Allahabad, Kanpur, Farrukhabad, Haridwar, Devprayag. **3** False. In Bangladesh, 50 to 200 people are killed by tigers every year. **4** A yak.